LORENZO
The Naughty Parrot

LORENZO
The Naughty Parrot

Story by TONY JOHNSTON
Pictures by LEO POLITI

HARCOURT BRACE & COMPANY
Orlando Atlanta Austin Boston San Francisco Chicago Dallas New York
Toronto London

With thanks and *gracias*
to my inspirational editor, Allyn Johnston
—T. J.

This edition is published by special arrangement with Harcourt Brace
& Company.

Lorenzo the Naughty Parrot by Tony Johnston, illustrated by Leo Politi. Text
copyright © 1992 by Tony Johnston; illustrations copyright © 1992 by Leo
Politi. Reprinted by permission of Harcourt Brace & Company.

Printed in the United States of America

ISBN 0-15-302172-1

2 3 4 5 6 7 8 9 10   035   97 96 95 94 93

For my dear Juan Nicolás Rhoads,
who told me parrot stories
while the sun went down
and the tarantulas came out

and for Maury Shoemaker,
who showed me how to change the oil.

— T. J.

to all the
Boys and Girls
with affection

Leo Politi

THE BIRTHDAY PARTY

Lorenzo lived in a garden in Mexico. He was green as a leaf. When anyone came up the path, he flew out. He squawked loudly as if to say, "This is my garden. My house. My family. Behave yourself or answer to me."

He followed visitors to the door. He waited for the family to open it.

"*Gracias*, Lorenzo," they said. "Thank you."

"Squawk," said Lorenzo.

Then he marched back to the garden.

One day it was Ana's birthday. Everyone was excited. The children were excited because their friends were coming. Papa was excited because he had lost his wedding ring. It had always been loose. Today it had slipped off. Mama was excited because she had given it to him. Lorenzo was excited because everyone else was excited.

Papa looked under the sofa.

"*Ay-ay-ay,*" he groaned. "Where is that ring?"

"*Ay-ay-ay,*" muttered Lorenzo. He looked under the sofa, too.

"*Ay-ay-ay-ay-ay-ay-ay-ay!*" squawked Lorenzo. He was stuck.

Papa got him out.

The doorbell rang.

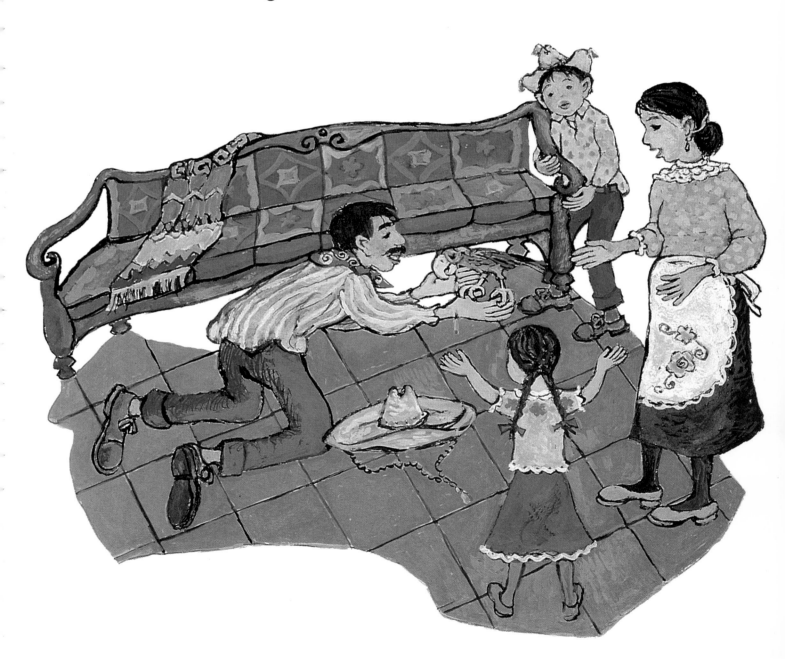

The friends were arriving for the party. Now Lorenzo had more important things to do than get stuck under furniture. He hurried to squawk at the friends.

He squawked loudly at each one as if to say, "This is my garden. My house. My family. Behave yourself or answer to me."

"Oh!" the friends cried. "This parrot is a real watchbird!"

Lorenzo decided he liked the friends.

But he did not like the presents they brought. He squawked at them instead. He gave them dirty looks.

The party began. Ana's brother, Diego, put the presents away. The children played games and ate. They hit the *piñata* and ate. They sang songs and ate some more.

Then it was time for presents. Papa went to get them.

"Ay-ay-ay!" cried Papa. "What is this?"

The presents were already open! Paper was everywhere.

The paper wiggled. Papa looked under it. There was Lorenzo, eating the party paper.

"You naughty bird," said Papa.

"He is not naughty," Ana said. "He was protecting us from the presents."

Everyone laughed and said, *"Gracias,* Lorenzo."

They sang the birthday song to Ana. Lorenzo screeched some notes he knew.

Everyone clapped.

"Feliz cumpleaños, Ana! Happy birthday!"

Then Lorenzo strutted back to the garden. He took a piece of party paper with him to chew on.

Papa had a car. A beautiful car. He called it *La Reina,* The Queen.

La Reina was long and shiny and sleek. La Reina was old, too. She always broke down. Papa loved her anyway.

He fixed La Reina with bits of wire. Or coils of rope. La Reina went a few more miles and broke down.

Papa changed her oil and gave her clean water. La Reina went a few more miles — and broke down again.

"You spoil her, Papa," the children said. "She repays you by breaking down."

"No, no, no," said Papa. "I spoil La Reina. So she goes a few more miles for me."

Papa liked cookies. Every day he drove to the bakery to buy some. Warm and fresh. He took the children with him. He took Lorenzo, too. On the way home they ate cookies. Papa put the rest in the cookie jar.

Each time he heard La Reina start up, Lorenzo hoped Papa was going for cookies. He hurried to the car, hopped through an open window, and sat on the seat beside Papa. Lorenzo was always ready for cookies.

One day Papa was in the garage. He was looking for his ring again. Ana and Diego were helping him. They rattled and shuffled and poked around. No one found the ring.

At last Papa said, "After so much work, we need cookies."

"*Sí*, Papa! We need cookies!" the children agreed.

"I'll get my hat," said Papa. He never drove La Reina without it.

The children ran for his hat.

Papa started up La Reina.

Lorenzo heard it. He hurried to the garage, hopped through the car window, and sat on the seat.

Uup. Uup. Uup. The motor coughed and stopped. Papa turned the key again. La Reina coughed again. She would not start.

"Something is wrong with La Reina," said Papa. "I will fix her. First, I will change the oil. Oil can never be too clean."

Lorenzo followed Papa. He did just what Papa did.

Papa took the oil pan and put it under La Reina. Lorenzo poked the oil pan with his beak. Papa loosened a plug with a wrench. Lorenzo pecked the plug.

Dirty oil dripped into the oil pan. Papa watched it.

Lorenzo perched on the edge of the pan. He watched the oil, too. He leaned over to watch it better. Over, over, over. And—

PLOP! He fell in.

"You naughty bird!" Papa said.

He fished Lorenzo out.

"*Niños!*" Papa called. "Children! Come! Lorenzo has taken an oil bath. Will you clean him, please?"

Ana and Diego tried to clean Lorenzo. But he was still dirty. The oil would take a long time to come off.

He hid behind big leaves in the garden. When anyone came up the path, he flapped out, brown as a bat. He squawked loudly as if to say, "This is my garden. My house. My family. Joke about my color and answer to me."

Then he stomped back behind the leaves.

CHRISTMAS EVE

It was Christmas Eve. The chimney was clogged.

But the family knew that a clogged chimney would not keep *San Nicolás,* Santa Claus, from coming. So everyone had sent him a Christmas list.

Papa wanted a wedding ring. Not a new one. He wanted the old one back.

Mama wanted a new floor. The old one was lumpy from many people coming in and going out. But a new floor would be hard for San Nicolás to bring. Instead, Mama asked for a shawl.

Diego and Ana wrote *juguetes,* toys, on their lists. Then they added *por favor.* Please helps everything.

The children hung up their stockings. They left punch and cookies for San Nicolás. They kissed Mama and Papa and went to bed — with their eyes wide open. They hoped if they did that their eyes would stay open all night and they would see San Nicolás.

The children did that each year. It never worked.

Everyone was fast asleep. The house was quiet as quiet.

Then — there was a strange noise in the garden. It was not La Reina coughing. It was not the wind blowing the trees. Someone was coming up the path dragging something heavy. A big bag.

Lorenzo flew out squawking as if to say, "This is my garden. My house. My family. Behave yourself or answer to me."

San Nicolás (for that is who it was) understood.

"I will behave myself very well," he said. And he did.

He looked so kindly that Lorenzo let him go inside. Still, Lorenzo watched him. He watched the bag, too. He did not trust it one bit.

San Nicolás stuffed the stockings with good things. Lorenzo watched that bag. San Nicolás set out presents. Lorenzo bit the bag. San Nicolás drank some punch. He tasted a cookie. Lorenzo would have liked to taste a cookie, but he tasted the bag instead. And he tugged it. Hard.

He fell down, the bag tore open, and something poured out all over the floor. Sunflower seeds.

San Nicolás chuckled. "So you have found what I brought for you," he said.

By now Lorenzo liked San Nicolás very much. He was sorry he had torn the bag.

San Nicolás knew that. Gently, he held out a finger. Lorenzo hopped onto it. Then San Nicolás took Lorenzo to the garden, set him down among the leaves, and went on his way.

The next morning everyone hurried to the living room. They saw the presents.

Papa got a fancy cap to wear when he drove La Reina. Mama got a fine shawl. She wore it to breakfast. Ana and Diego got toys. And, as everyone could see, Lorenzo got sunflower seeds.

Ana saw something else. It was a plate with a big cookie on it. On top of the cookie was a note. The note said:

> Dear Lorenzo,
>   Thank you for watching my bag.
>   You never know about bags. This cookie is for you.
>   *Feliz Navidad,* San Nicolás.

"*Feliz Navidad!*" everyone cried.
"Merry Christmas!"

THE NEW FLOOR

Papa was a brickmaker. He made beautiful red bricks in a big oven behind the house.

Papa knew Mama wanted a new floor.

He said, "I will make Mama a new floor. It will be the smoothest floor anywhere."

He mixed the mortar near the oven in the backyard. Ana and Diego saw Papa. They came to help. Lorenzo saw Papa. He came to help, too.

Papa took a wooden mold and shaped the thick mortar into bricks. He slid them from the mold one by one. One by one. Lorenzo watched.

The children turned the fresh bricks on their sides to harden before Papa baked them in the oven. Lorenzo turned his head to one side to admire them.

When the last brick was shaped, Papa took a twig. He scratched something on the brick.

"What did you write?" Diego asked.

"My initials," said Papa. "That brick will go in one corner. It will remind Mama of just who made the smoothest floor anywhere."

They left the bricks to set and went inside for lunch.

When Papa came back to bake them, something was different. The bricks were knocked over. And they were not smooth anymore. There were footprints all over them! Funny, scratchy footprints.

"Lorenzo, you naughty bird!" Papa cried.

"He is not naughty," said the children. "He did what you did."

"But I scratched *one* brick," said Papa. "Lorenzo scratched *all* of them!"

Then Papa laughed.

"It's not so bad," he said. "We will turn them over. The new floor will still be smooth."

"No, no, no," Mama said. She had heard the commotion and come outside. "I want my floor with the footprints showing. It will remind me of Lorenzo when I am working. It will make me smile."

"Then that is what you shall have," Papa said. "The roughest floor in Mexico."

Soon the floor was ready. *Los abuelitos,* the grandparents, came to see it. Papa bought cookies to celebrate.

Grandma and Grandpa walked up the path. Lorenzo flew out. He squawked loudly as if to say, "This is my garden. My house. My family. Behave yourselves or answer to me."

Grandma and Grandpa always behaved themselves. And they always jumped when Lorenzo flew out. Then they laughed.

"Ay, Lorenzo! Ay-ay-ay!"

When they saw the new floor, they laughed harder still.

"What a nice pattern!" cried Grandpa.

"It is the prettiest floor I ever saw," said Grandma.

Lorenzo strutted in a circle all around it.

"Now everyone needs cookies," said Mama. "Please help yourselves."

So everyone ate cookies and admired the floor.

Lorenzo hopped up on the cookie jar. He reached down to help himself. Deep, deep, down. And he found—Papa's wedding ring!

The family cheered. Papa gave Lorenzo the biggest cookie in the jar.

"You are the best bird I know," he said.

Lorenzo squawked loudly as if to say, "Of course I am."

Then he swaggered back to the garden with the cookie. And he ate it all up.

The illustrations and hand-lettering in this book
were done in watercolors and ink on illustration board.